Searchlight Books™

Hunting and Fishing

Deep-Sea Fishing

Kyle Brach

Lerner Publications ◆ Minneapolis

Lerner Publications Company
An imprint of Lerner Publishing Group, Inc.
241 First Avenue North
Minneapolis, MN 55401 USA

For reading levels and more information, look up this title at www.lernerbooks.com.

Main body text set in Adrianna Regular.
Typeface provided by Chank.

Library of Congress Cataloging-in-Publication Data

Names: Brach, Kyle, author.
Title: Deep-sea fishing / Kyle Brach.
Description: Minneapolis, MN, USA : Lerner Publications, an imprint of Lerner Publishing Group, Inc., [2024] | Series: Searchlight books. Hunting and fishing | Includes bibliographical references and index. | Audience: Ages 8–11 | Audience: Grades 4–6 | Summary: "Could you catch a fish that's at least 100 feet below the water's surface? In deep-sea fishing, fishers do just that. Discover the kinds of fish fishers look for, the gear fishers use, and more"— Provided by publisher.
Identifiers: LCCN 2022049928 (print) | LCCN 2022049929 (ebook) | ISBN 9781728491554 (lib. bdg.) | ISBN 9798765603741 (pbk.) | ISBN 9798765600399 (eb pdf)
Subjects: LCSH: Big game fishing—Juvenile literature.
Classification: LCC SH457.5 .B73 2024 (print) | LCC SH457.5 (ebook) | DDC 799.16—dc23/eng/20221118

LC record available at https://lccn.loc.gov/2022049928
LC ebook record available at https://lccn.loc.gov/2022049929

Manufactured in the United States of America
1-CG-7/15/23

Table of Contents

Chapter 1

WHAT IS DEEP-SEA FISHING?

The boat drifts slowly with your rod in the holder at the back of the boat, called a stern. The wind blows in your face, and you smell the salty air. You feel like adventure is just ahead. Sure enough, your line pulls. You caught a fish! You pull the rod out of the holder and let the line run. The fight begins.

Welcome to deep-sea fishing! It's one of the most exciting fishing adventures, where the fish are bigger, faster, stronger, and more difficult to catch.

A FAMILY DEEP-SEA FISHING.

Schools of fish swim below a fishing boat.

Deep-sea fishing happens miles away from an ocean shore. It requires strong and flexible fishing rods, and a reel that can hold a lot of line. After all, deep-sea anglers hope to catch fish that weigh from 20 to 400 pounds (9.1 to 181.4 kg). Finding the type of fish they want to catch depends on getting their boat in the right place at the right time of day.

Fishing History

While humans have been fishing in lakes, rivers, and near ocean shorelines for at least 165,000 years, scientists believed that we had only been deep-sea fishing for 12,000 years. That changed in 2011, when researchers made a remarkable discovery in a cave on East Timor, an island north of Australia. They found 42,000-year-old bones from tuna and parrotfish, which are typically found in deep waters, suggesting that humans there were deep-sea fishing a lot earlier than scientists thought.

East Timor is an island country in Southeast Asia.

Types of Fish

There are hundreds of types of fish you can catch when deep-sea fishing. What you find depends on where you are fishing: the Atlantic Ocean, the Pacific Ocean, or the Gulf of Mexico. The most sought-after fish include the blue marlin, which can grow up to 14 feet (4.3 m) long and weigh up to 2,000 pounds (907.2 kg). Swordfish, sailfish, bluefin tuna, and mako sharks are other big catches anglers would love to make.

Blue marlins are predators and a popular catch for anglers.

Mahi-mahi means "strong" in the Hawaiian language.

Smaller fish to catch include the dorado, also called the mahi-mahi fish, which can weigh up to 50 pounds (22.7 kg), and red snapper, which can weigh 20 pounds (9.1 kg) or more.

There is space for many anglers on deep-sea party boats.

The Right Stuff

To catch these bigger, faster fish, you need the right gear. When first starting out, you might book a spot on a party boat. These are large boats that can hold fifty to a hundred or more people, and they often rent most, if not all the gear you'll need to get started. You fish from a spot on the boat, and although it may seem crowded, it's a great way to learn about fishing while watching others.

Chartering a boat is more expensive, but it reserves a private boat for just your family and friends to use. Do your research and find an experienced captain who knows the best places in that area for deep-sea fishing.

Finding a boat captain who knows a lot about deep-sea fishing is key to a good charter boat experience.

Tackle

Tackle is the name for all the gear you need to fish, including your rod, reel, hooks, lures, sinkers, fishing line, and a net. As a general rule, saltwater tackle needs to be made of higher quality materials than freshwater tackle. After all, the fish are bigger, and the water is rougher.

Different lures attract different types of fish.

Offshore fishing rods must be flexible and strong.

Rod, Reel, and Line

Your rod and reel hold the line that you'll use to cast your bait. Graphite or fiberglass rods are strong and also bend easily. The reel is attached to the rod and is used for releasing the line and then reeling it back in. You attach a hook to the line to snag a fish. If using live bait, you'll attach it to your hook. Artificial bait called lures can be used. Your fishing line must be strong enough so it doesn't snap.

Chapter 2

PLAYING IT SAFE

The captain of your charter or party boat will check the weather for the day. If you're going fishing on your own boat, you must know what is predicted. Offshore weather conditions can change rapidly, so stay alert and monitor the weather. Delay your trip if there's a storm heading your way or if you see lightning or really big waves.

Watch What You Wear

You're going to be out on open water for hours, so don't forget to protect yourself from the sun. You need a hat

Rubber soled shoes provide traction on wet boat surfaces.

with a strap (so it doesn't blow off), sunglasses to protect against the glare of the sun from the water, and plenty of sunscreen.

Your outer layer of clothing should be waterproof, and your shoes should have good traction for the slippery deck of the boat. Finally, bring extra clothes in case you get really wet. Wearing a personal floatation device, or life jacket, when on the water is a must.

Stay aware of other anglers in the boat before casting a line.

Sharp and Slippery

Make sure not to grab a line with a fish on it without a heavy-duty pair of fishing gloves. Slippery fish are hard to handle. Be sure to watch out for the hooks. Also, watch out for fish with teeth. Don't put your fingers in a fish's mouth unless you know for certain it is safe.

Always know what is behind you before you cast your line. You don't want your hook getting caught on anything or anyone.

STEM Spotlight

Seasickness can take the fun out of fishing. The up and down motion of the boat makes you dizzy and nauseated. Your inner ear has tubes filled with fluid that send information about balance and movement. Motion sickness happens when your inner ear and eyes send different messages to your brain. When your ears say you're moving and your eyes say you're not, your brain gets confused, and you feel sick.

Chapter 3

DEEP-SEA FISHING BASICS

The basics of fishing are simple: you're trying to fool fish into thinking your bait or lure is food. The fish bites, and you reel it in. But you must know where the fish are going to be, and the best way to fool them. New fishers rely on information about where fish are biting from more experienced anglers and ship captains.

What Fish Eat

Knowing what a fish likes to eat gives you a good idea of what to bait your hook with. For instance, bluefish are not fussy eaters and will go for fresh bait or lures. Atlantic cod, however, prefer a large piece of clam on your hook.

Some big fish eat small fish, worms, and crustaceans.

The Best Fishing Conditions

Fish will be found wherever there is food for them. Tide and current can affect the food's location. Fishing is best during the first hour when the tide changes and water levels begin to rise or drop. Morning and evening are also great times to fish because this is when fish are looking for food.

Early morning is a good time to catch fish looking for food.

A FISHING BOAT TROLLS THE WATER WAITING FOR FISH TO BITE.

Trolling

Trolling involves motoring your boat slowly with your line in the water at the stern of the boat. With the bait dragging behind the boat, you might get the attention of a swordfish, sailfish, or big tuna.

This fish finder shows a school of fish swimming nearby.

Bottom Fishing

Some anglers use a fish finder that shows you how deep the water is. It also reveals objects like coral reefs and shipwrecks where fish like to eat and hide. If a captain has an idea of where a school of fish might be, they may turn off the boat and drop the anchor. You drop your line straight to the ocean floor and wait. This is called bottom fishing.

Drifting

Drifting is similar to bottom fishing, except the anchor isn't dropped. The boat simply drifts with the current.

An angler drifting at sea

Hauling in a big fish takes a lot of strength.

Hauling In Your Catch

With patience, and perhaps a little bit of luck, you may get a bite. Reeling in a deep-sea fish can be a struggle. That's why it's called a fight! You can use a harness around your waist to secure your pole.

First, you set the hook in the fish's mouth by pointing your rod tip toward the fish and then sweeping it quickly to the side. Next, you might let the fish run the line to tire it. Then, with the line high, you reel it in. The fish may thrash, jump, and circle to get free, but remain patient. Have someone help bring the fish onboard with a landing net.

Sometimes anglers must strap themselves into a fighting chair while reeling in big fish.

Chapter 4

CONSERVATION

Deep-sea fishing depends on clean oceans and healthy fish. Government agencies set regulations for the size of fish you can keep, how many you can fish, and which species are off-limits. Responsible anglers know the rules and follow them. This helps ensure that species aren't overfished, and endangered species are left alone.

Anglers must do their part to protect oceans from pollution.

Make sure you have a proper license or permit to fish. The money spent on this helps support education programs and conservation efforts. Of course, don't throw anything in the water. Be sure to properly dispose of fishing line, old hooks and lures, and food packaging.

Catch and Release

If you don't plan on eating the fish you catch, release it back in the ocean, but safely. Make sure it is unharmed first. Then wet your hands before you handle it and quickly remove the hook before sliding the fish back in the water. If it's really tired, move it gently through the water as it recovers.

By practicing good conservation, people will be able to enjoy deep-sea fishing for many years to come.

Responsible anglers help conserve fish.

Fishing Tips

- Let other people help you the first time you catch a fish. You may need more than one person to help you get the fish onto the boat.
- Do research before chartering a boat or buying a spot on a party boat.
- Clean the saltwater off your rod, reel, lures, and hooks.
- Take every precaution to stay safe on the water. Talk about what to do if someone goes overboard.

Hosing down fishing gear and boats removes saltwater that corrodes metal.

Glossary

angler: a fisher

bait: real or human-made food used to attract fish

catch and release: gently returning a fish back in the water after catching it

charter: a private boat you can rent to go deep-sea fishing

fish finder: a sonar depth-finder used to find schools of fish in the sea

lure: artificial bait made to look like or move like real fish food

party boat: a boat that takes passengers deep-sea fishing for the day, and usually provides equipment needed for fishing

sinker: a weight tied to a line that keeps the bait from floating

tackle: the name for all the gear needed for fishing

traction: use of materials that aid in the resistance of a shoe sliding across a slippery surface

Learn More

Bell, Samantha. *Deep Sea Fisher: 12 Things to Know.* Mankato, MN: 12-Story Library, 2022.

Britannica Kids: Deep-Sea Life
https://kids.britannica.com/students/article/deep-sea-life/273947

Britannica Kids: Fishing
https://kids.britannica.com/students/article/fishing/274328

TakeMeFishing.org: Everything You Need to Start Fishing
https://www.takemefishing.org/how-to-fish/fishing-resources-events/everything-you-need-to-start-fishing

Mazzarella, Kerri. *Deep Sea Fishing.* New York: Crabtree Publishing, 2023.

Reeves, Diane Lindsey. *Freshwater Fishing.* Minneapolis: Lerner Publications, 2024.

Index

Photo Acknowledgments

Image Credits: p.5; Lawrence Weslowski Jr/Dreamstime, p.6; sylvae/Shutterstock, p. 7; Atosan/Shutterstock, p. 8; Corey A Ford/Dreamstime, p. 9; Jason Richeux/Shutterstock, p. 10; FotosForTheFuture/Shutterstock, p. 11; Anthony Aneese Totah Jr/Dreamstime, p. 12; stammphoto/iStock Photos, p. 13; Sompransong Khrueaphan/Shutterstock, p. 15; Kateryna Onyshchuk/Shutterstock, p. 16; Sebastian Czapnik/Dreamstime, p. 17; Kopitinphoto/Dreamstime, p. 19; mcmortgreen/Shutterstock, p. 20; Justin Klusener Photos/Shutterstock, p. 21; Ivansabo/Dreamstime, p. 22; Johanna Goodyear/Dreamstime, p. 23; AS_Photos/iStock Photos, p. 24; Maridav/Shutterstock, p. 25; Meisterphotos/Dreamstime, p. 27; Romolo Tavini/Dreamstime, p. 28; Susan Montgomery/Shutterstock, p. 29; George P. Choma/Shutterstock.

Cover: martinedoucet/iStockPhotos.